ST. ANTHONY

Finding Your Financial Joy

A 30-DAY MEDITATION
AND JOURNAL WORKBOOK

ST. ANTHONY

Finding Your Financial Joy

A 30-DAY MEDITATION AND JOURNAL WORKBOOK

SHIRA PLOTZKER

Edited by **Denise Kojak**

Copyright © 2012 by SHIRA PLOTZKER

DISCLAIMER

Please note this book is designed to provide information only. This information is provided and sold with the knowledge that the publisher and author do not offer any legal or other professional advice.

Shira Plotzker is not affiliated with any religious group, church, synagogue or other spiritual center. The information herein is not from a church or religious group. The opinions expressed in this book are not meant to diagnose and/or cure any medical symptoms. If you are having any issues, medical or otherwise, it is always best to consult with the appropriate medical or other professional.

This book contains information intended to educate and entertain. Neither Shira Plotzker nor her associates assume any liability for any misunderstanding in the intended messages in this book.

Every effort has been made to make this book as accurate as possible. It is written the way the information was received. This book should serve as a general guide and not as the ultimate source of subject information.

This book is designed to provide information as channeled through the author from St. Anthony and does not purport to contain all information available on St. Anthony nor has it been created to be specific to any individual's or organizations' situations or needs.

DEDICATION

This book is dedicated to St. Anthony.

Thank you for giving me this book to give out to the Readers and The World.

Thank you for changing my life.

ACKNOWLEDGEMENTS

Above all, thank you Mother Mary for calling me to do this work. I am Humbled, Honored and Blessed by all you do for me.

A very special thank you to Denise Kojak. Thank you for your friendship, talent, time, and gifts. Thank you for editing this work!

Also, thank you to: Ariann Thomas, Deana Valente, and Arlene Rosenberg for all of your support. I appreciate all.

A very special thank you to Monica Meaux Hope. http://www.monicahope.com/

Lastly, thank you to all my clients and friends.

TABLE OF CONTENTS

AUTHOR PREFACE

I am a Psychic, Medium and Pet Communicator. In 1998, I started to have visions of Mother Mary. That would not be so interesting, except that I am Jewish. I didn't even know who she was. At first, I asked, "Who are you"? And she replied, "I am Mother Mary." Then I asked, "Why are you here"? And she replied, "I am the one who calls you to do this work." Finally, I asked, "Why"? And she said, "Because you said you would answer."

After having visions of Mother Mary, I began to channel information from the Spirit World. I found that when I put my hands on the computer keyboard, the words seemed to appear as I was typing. I was not aware of the words that were forming as I typed. It was only after I was done typing that I was able to read the words written on the computer screen.

The information or "wisdom" in this book was given to me to share with you. I am unable to do this work on my own. It is only in the interest of giving you, the reader, this information that I've written this book.

This work was channeled through me by St. Anthony.

INTRODUCTION

FROM ST. ANTHONY

This is my second book for you. My first book was about finding or locating all that you would need to enjoy. This new book is all about finding financial joy.

I am Channeling this book through Shira. It is incredible that other Saints and I are able to do this for you.

Each day is a Channeled Meditation with several inspirational thoughts. The Journal Workbook Pages contain three inspirational questions.

Please read this book at your own pace. Some people like to read the meditation and inspirational thoughts in the morning and journal in the evening.

There is no right or wrong way to read this book. Please go at a pace that feels comfortable or right for you.

If you feel thirsty while reading this book, it is perfectly natural and normal. You may want to have a glass of water near you as you read this work. If you do not feel thirsty, no worries. This is fine, too.

We hope you will enjoy all of our works.

Love,

St. Anthony

DAY 1

Financial Joy

Did you lose your financial joy? If so, I am the Saint for you. If you are reading this book, you may have lost your financial joy. And if you did, you may now ask me, St. Anthony, to find it for you. If you're not sure how to do this, just say to yourself or out loud, "St. Anthony, please find my Financial Joy for me." And I will. After all, I am the Saint of all lost things.

Today,

Ask me to find your financial Joy. (Do not ask for money to pay your bills), ask for Financial Joy.

What would bring you joy today? If you're not sure, just think of one of your favorite things or colors. You have just found your joy.

Now, add money to it.

How does this feel?

QUESTION 1:

Financial Joy is about being in your rightful place. Are you in your "rightful" place with money? How do you know? It just feels right. Today, see yourself feeling right with money. I, St. Anthony, am happy to find this for you. After all, I am The Saint of All Lost Things. How does this feel? Please write down any thoughts or comments you may have here:

_____

_____

_____

_____

QUESTION 2:

Now that you have found your rightful place with money, what, if anything, is different or feels different? Please write down any thoughts or comments you may have here:

_____

_____

_____

_____

QUESTION 3:

Did you notice that you are no longer telling yourself what you did wrong? And, does it feel joyful? If so, I, St. Anthony, was glad to Find this for you. After all, I am the Saint of All Lost Things. If you would like, you may ask yourself, "How does this feel?" Please write down any thoughts or comments you may have here:

_____

_____

_____

_____

DAY 2

Trust

Today, I, St. Anthony, am going to bring you financial joy. When I bring you something, I also find it for you. I can do this for you. After all, I am the Saint of all lost things.

You may say to yourself or out loud, "St. Anthony, I trust in you." And, now, you have found your financial joy within.

Today,

Count how many times you asked me, St. Anthony, to bring you financial joy.

How does this feel?

Now, look around and see how many things you have that have brought you financial joy.

You are no longer looking to buy things with your money. You have found your financial joy. The joy is in having financial joy, not what money can buy for you.

This *is* your new financial revelation!

QUESTION 1:

Who do you trust financially? Have you lost your faith or trust? G-d* Has a Trust-fund for you. And it all starts with trust. I will find yours for you. Just say to yourself or out loud, "G-d, I Trust in You." And, I will find your trust-fund. How does this feel? Please write down any thoughts or comments you may have here:

_____

_____

_____

_____

*Being Jewish, I do not Use the "o" in G-d. The reason is that I do not use G-d's Name in Vain. If I put in an "o", and the word was ripped up or destroyed, it would be using His Name in Vain. This is just my own Personal Belief. If you would like, please add the "o" back in.

Also, if you would like to use a different word ("Spirit", "Universe", or any other Word), please feel free to use a Word that works well for you.

QUESTION 2:

Are you looking for happiness by buying things to fill a void? This is not financial joy! This is "ROBBERY"! What are you depriving or robbing yourself of instead of having financial joy?

Please write down any thoughts or comments you may have here:

_____

_____

_____

_____

QUESTION 3:

Now, please ask me, St. Anthony, to give you, or to find you financial joy. Some of us are so good at asking for things, yet we never ask for financial joy. Today, ask for financial joy. Say out loud or to yourself, "St. Anthony, please find me financial joy. Please find my rightful place with money and show me where my "trust-fund" is." How does this feel? Please write down any comments or thoughts you may have here:

_____

_____

_____

_____

BONUS QUESTION:

Now, allow your financial joy into your life. You can do this by saying to yourself or out loud, "I now allow my financial joy into my life." How does that feel? Please write down any thoughts or comments you may have here:

_____

_____

_____

_____

DAY 3

Financial Transcendence

Did you know that being who you are, pays off your bills? When did you try to be "something else" or "someone else"? This is when you started to treat yourself as "less than." This is when you first felt like "less than." This is when you told yourself you were not good enough. And you stopped being joyful. It had nothing to do with money at all.

What "financial situation" would you like to rise above today? If you have any answer(s) to this question, you are ready to transcend. Let's do our financial Transcend Dance! When you are lifted above this situation, you will dance! This is true transcendence! Are you dancing, or are you complaining?

If you are looking to pay off your bills, see yourself celebrating instead! And let your celebration begin now! Your celebration pays off your bills. Today,

15

dance into transcendence with me! You are no longer the wallflower. You are radiant in your magnificence. How do I know this? I have just found it for you. You see, I AM the Saint of all lost things!

Today,

Let's celebrate!

Let's be radiant in our radiance.

"How?", you may ask.

Just smile!

And, if you are daring, you might want to say this phrase out loud or to yourself: "Thinking about my money makes me smile!" (But only if you are daring!)

QUESTION 1:

Are you ready to do your financial happy dance? What would that even look or feel like? Please write any thoughts or comments you may have here:

_____

_____

_____

_____

QUESTION 2:

Are you doing your financial transcendence Happy Dance?!?! Are you feeling radiant today? If not, you may ask me, St. Anthony, to find your radiance. Just think of one thing that makes you smile. This *IS* your true radiance. How does this feel? Please write down any comments you may have here:

_____

_____

_____

_____

QUESTION 3:

You're no longer using money to make yourself feel less than. How does that feel? Did you feel the financial joy? Please write down any thoughts or comments you may have here:

_____

_____

_____

_____

DAY 4

Debt

Some people think that debt is what they owe. Debt is not what you owe. Debt is the part of you that you do not like. Debt reflects what you do not like. Now, let's polish him or her up! He or she may have lost their honor. Just take out your debt – and look at him or her very closely. And say, "I honor you." If that doesn't work, and it may not, just say to yourself or out loud, "I'm sorry I didn't honor you, or myself." And then you may ask me, St. Anthony, to find your honor for you. Simply say to yourself or out loud, "St. Anthony, please find my honor for me." And I will. After all, I am the Saint of all lost things.

Today,

Honor the people who didn't honor you. And in that, you will find your honor.

(If you cannot honor these people, please go to Day 5 to see Forgiveness).

Honor honors, or is Honest; it does not forgive.

Your honor brings you financial well-being.

QUESTION 1:

Did you honor or did you Blame yourself today? Honor cannot blame. Now you know the truth. How does this feel? Please write down any thoughts or comments you may have here:

_____

_____

_____

_____

QUESTION 2:

Your Honor honors you. How does this feel? Please write down any thoughts or comments you may have here:

_____

_____

_____

_____

QUESTION 3:

How would it feel to be honored? I, St. Anthony, Honor you. I always have. How does this feel? Please write down any thoughts or comments you may have here:

_____

_____

_____

_____

BONUS QUESTION:

Now, debt is no longer an issue or a reflection of you. Honor is. How does this feel? Please write down any thoughts or comments you may have here:

_____

_____

_____

_____

DAY 5

Forgiveness

Yesterday, we talked about Honor. You cannot have honor without forgiveness. Just try it. Try to honor when you are angry. You cannot. In the Ten Commandments – It says Honor your Mother and Father. You lose your honor when you cannot forgive. And now I, St. Anthony, will find your honor for you as you forgive. You can also ask me to find your forgiveness for you. And I will.

With forgiveness comes joy. You see, when you forgive, you are no longer dependent upon what others say or do. And you start to trust yourself again. And this trust is your trust-fund. And in your trust-fund is honor. Forgiveness opens the door to honor. And honor allows.

Today,

See your forgiveness leading you to honor.

Did you remember to ask me, St. Anthony, to find your forgiveness for you?

If so, point to the place within that you keep it.

Forgiveness is your "SAFE." You now have a SAFE place.

This is where you put your financial joy: in your safe of Forgiveness and Honor.

QUESTION 1:

You now have access to your honor within. Count how many ways you can use this new honor today! Please write down any thoughts or comments you may have here:

_____

_____

_____

_____

QUESTION 2:

If you would like, you can think of the things that you no longer tell yourself now that you have honor. What do you tell yourself now? Can you feel the smiles light up from within you? How does this feel? Please write down any thoughts or comments you may have here:

_____

_____

_____

_____

QUESTION 3:

Today, be proud of who you are. This is part of your new honor. How does this feel? Please write down any thoughts or comments you may have here:

_____

_____

_____

_____

DAY 6

Good Financial Choices

Did you make a good financial choice today? Did you know that your choice(s) led you here, directly to me, St. Anthony? When you make "wrong" choices, you start to blame yourself. And this blame erodes or eats away at your honor. Today, ask me, St. Anthony, to find all of your right choices. And I will. You didn't lose them at all. They've been here all along. And I was glad to find them for you. After all, I am the Saint of all lost things.

Please tell yourself that you made a good financial choice today and see what happens. Making good choices appreciates or adds to your honor. How does this feel?

Did you know that good financial choices start with allowing? Just say to yourself or out loud: "I am allowed to _____ (and fill in the blank).

33

Today,

Please say to yourself or out loud, "My good financial choices add to my honor."

If you're not sure where your good choices are, you may say to yourself or out loud, "St. Anthony, please find my financial good choices for me."

Honor your good choices, for they will honor you.

Now, say to yourself or out loud, "My good choices honor me."

QUESTION 1:

Today, tell yourself that you made a good financial choice and see what happens. Making good choices, appreciates or adds to your honor. How does this feel? Please write down any thoughts or comments you may have here:

_____

_____

_____

_____

QUESTION 2:

I, St. Anthony, have found your new Financial choices for you. Thank yourself for having the courage to make GREAT financial choices today! How does this feel? Please write down any thoughts or comments you may have here:

_____

_____

_____

_____

QUESTION 3:

Your newfound courage has given you a new AWE! How does this feel? Please write down any thoughts or comments you may have here:

_____

_____

_____

_____

BONUS QUESTION:

You have now found your awesomeness within. How does this feel? Please write down any thoughts or comments you may have here:

_____

_____

_____

_____

DAY 7

Rest

Rest. On every Seventh day, we rest.

Did you rest today?

Are you restless?

Ok, rest.

QUESTION 1:

Rest – Will you allow yourself to rest? Please write down any thoughts or comments you may have here:

_____

_____

_____

_____

QUESTION 2:

What would you like me, St. Anthony, to find you so that you can rest? If you would like, you may write any thoughts or comments you have here:

_____

_____

_____

_____

QUESTION 3:

What restful thoughts would you like to tell yourself today? If you would like, you may write any thoughts or comments you have here:

_____

_____

_____

_____

DAY 8

Allowing!

Today, ask yourself what you are allowed to have. What answers, if any, did you get? You might be very surprised. Did you know that good financial choices come with "allowing"? Let's all give our "allowance" (what we think we can have) back. And now we can really allow! What would happen if your financial choices allowed you to have more? What would that look like? Want to find out? Just ask, me, St. Anthony, to find it for you. And I will. After all, I am the Saint of all lost things. And I would love to find new ways of allowing especially for you!

Today,

Ask to be congratulated and watch your debt disappear. You have passed the test with flying colors! And I, St. Anthony, have found all the reasons for you to feel good about your financial accomplishments today! This was part of your financial joy. And I was able to find it for you. After all, I AM the Saint of all lost items.

Say to yourself or out loud, "My good financial choices allow me to have more!"

QUESTION 1:

Why didn't you allow yourself to have today? No need to answer. That's old news! How does this feel? Please write down any thoughts or comments you may have here:

_____

_____

_____

_____

QUESTION 2:

You just made a good financial choice. What did you get? (If you're not sure, you can just say, "More money!") How did this feel? Please write down any thoughts or comments you may have here:

_____

_____

_____

_____

QUESTION 3:

Allowing starts with asking! Please start to ask for more! How does this feel? Please write down any thoughts or comments you may have here:

_____

_____

_____

_____

DAY 9

Financial Anger

Are you financially angry? Do you have financial anger? If so, I am the Saint for you! When you are joyful, you are no longer angry. I bet you didn't know that. Financial joy and financial anger cannot coexist. Who are you existing with, in anger, that will not allow you to have joy? For Shira, the author, the answer was her debt. The anger around her would not allow her to have financial joy.

This *is* your wake-up call! Your debt has sounded the alarm! Now, shut the alarm off and allow joy into your life. It's all there waiting for you. I have found it for you! After all, I am the Saint of all lost things! I love you, St. Anthony.

Today,

Are you living in anger, fear or love?

If you answered "anger" or "fear," ask me, St. Anthony, to find the love for you.

Just remember this – anger and fear withhold.

Love allows.

QUESTION 1:

If you have anger, do not be alarmed. Just ask
yourself what you needed instead. People who get
what they need say, "thank you." Today, say,
"Thank you." How does this feel? Please write
down any thoughts or comments you may have
here:

_____

_____

_____

_____

QUESTION 2:

Are you still blaming? Anger blames. Do not blame others for your unmet expectations. Tell others what you need or expect. And see what happens next. You may be pleasantly surprised. How does this feel? Please write down any thoughts or comments you may have here:

_____

_____

_____

_____

QUESTION 3:

The next time you get angry, do not look to be right. Think of what you needed and ask yourself if you asked for it. You have now taken back your power! How does this feel? Please write down any thoughts or comments you may have here:

_____

_____

_____

_____

DAY 10

Asking!

Financially ask. What did you ask for (if anything) financially? If you asked for nothing, guess what: you got nothing! Now, ask again. Now ask for financial Joy. Just say, "St. Anthony, please find me Financial joy." You may feel your sadness or hurt well up within you as you hear or read these words. Do not be "alarmed" or upset. This is what was covering your financial joy! You just located your financial joy. It was underneath all that other stuff! And it was my pleasure to do this for you! You asked, you got, and you received! The first part was up to you; the second and third parts were done by us! I have helped you to find your ability to Financially Ask, Financially Get and Financially Receive today. I am able to do that for you. After all, I am the Saint of all lost things.

Today,

Did you ask or did you complain?

(Just as a for-your-information reminder, we are not the complaint department.)

Thank you for asking!

QUESTION 1:

What did you financially ask for? And did you do it with joy? How does this feel? Please write down any thoughts or comments you may have here:

_____

_____

_____

_____

QUESTION 2:

Are you waiting for an answer? Or are you expecting to receive? Can you feel the difference? Please, write down any thoughts or comments you may have here:

_____

_____

_____

_____

QUESTION 3:

Did you feel sad or upset? If so, no need to worry at all. Beneath feeling sad or upset is the Joy. Please ask for *what you wanted us to give you* instead. Do not ask for what you wanted to *have*. Ask us for what *we wanted to give you.* Sometimes, we take things so that we can give you something way so much better! How does this feel? Please write any thoughts or comments you may have here... If you didn't feel upset or sad, please feel free to add your own thoughts or comments below:

_____

_____

_____

_____

DAY 11

Financially Ask and Receive

Who or what did you give to Financially? Did you pay a bill? Did you curse that you didn't have the money to pay it in full? Did your stomach tie itself into knots as you opened up yet another unpaid bill? Or, did your stomach tie itself into knots as you paid another bill? If so, you are now ready to receive. Today, ask to financially receive. Guess what? When you ask to receive, you get. When you ask to financially receive, you get money.

You can now ask me, St. Anthony, to find you money; not more money, but... MONEY: LUSCIOUS, DELIGHTFUL, ENJOYABLE, MONEY! And I will. I will find you so much money as long as you tell me that are going to enjoy it! I can do this for you, and I will. You see, I am the Saint of all lost things. And it would be my pleasure to do this for you. I Love You. St. Anthony

Today,

Did you remember to ask for money? Or, did you ask to pay a bill?

When you have a lot of money, paying bills is not a concern.

QUESTION 1:

Did you ask for money or did you ask for more money? When you ask for more money it's about having enough. When you ask for money, you allow "more" money into your life. How does this feel? Please write down any thoughts or comments you may have here:

_____

_____

_____

_____

QUESTION 2:

Did you remember to expect to receive "more" money? Or can you just see or imagine an extra zero at the end of your bank account balance? How does this feel? Please write down any thoughts or comments you may have here:

_____

_____

_____

_____

QUESTION 3:

Are you beginning to see money as luscious and amazing now? How does this feel? Please write down any thoughts or comments you may have here:

_____

_____

_____

_____

DAY 12

Financial Value

All is Financially Divine. I see the Financial Divine in you. I honor the Financial Divine in you. I honor your financial mistakes. I honor your financial achievements. I honor your Financial life. I honor the way you financially love. I honor you financially. It is an honor to financially know you. I value you financially. I value your life financially. I value your financial ideas. I value your financial way of loving. You have a safe and loving financial place, here with me, St. Anthony.

You are G-d's Planted seed! And you are going to break through the soil to grow in this rich, Divine, Fertile, Blessed, Loving, and Financial way! And now, all is Financially Divine. I can find this for you. All you had to do was ask. After all, I am the Saint of all lost things!

Today,

Did you see the Divine in yourself today?
I, St. Anthony, saw it. And it was Divine!

QUESTION 1:

What would you do if you saw money as Divine? How does this feel? Please write down any thoughts or comments you may have here:

_____

_____

_____

_____

QUESTION 2:

If you made a financial mistake (not that you did) could you forgive yourself? How does this feel? Please write down any thoughts or comments you may have here:

_____

_____

_____

_____

QUESTION 3:

Did you know that all forgiveness, even of yourself, leads you to greater love and prosperity? How does this feel? Please, write down any thoughts or comments you may have here:

_____

_____

_____

_____

DAY 13

Financial Investment

Today, I will find your financial investments. Just say to yourself or out loud, "St. Anthony, please find my financial investments." And I will show you all the Financial Divine you've been missing out on! You see, you saw debt as a way to rise above any challenge. You may have seen your debt as an investment. You never saw our investment in you. Now, all is well and financially Divine. You are now financially stable and free. And I found it for you. After all, I am the Saint of all lost things.

Today,

Please say to yourself or out loud, "St. Anthony invested in me."

You deserve this.

QUESTION 1:

Please say to yourself or out loud, "St. Anthony, please invest in me." How did it feel? Please write down any thoughts or comments you may have here:

_____

_____

_____

_____

QUESTION 2:

Now, please say to yourself or out loud, "St. Anthony, please invest financially in me". And I, St. Anthony, will. How does this feel? Please write down any thoughts or comments you may have here:

_____

_____

_____

_____

QUESTION 3:

Now, if you are brave, you may say to yourself or out loud, "St. Anthony, please show me my investments." And; I will. How does this feel? Please write down any thoughts or comments you may have here: (Please note, if your stomach tightened up, do not be alarmed. Some of your investments may not have been good. No worries though, we'll discuss that on Day 15.)

_____

_____

_____

_____

DAY 14

Rest

Let's rest today. We can do the rest tomorrow.

Today,

If you are not resting, you are concerned. Let's write down all of our concerns. And rest.

QUESTION 1:

If you are concerned, write it down; see it being taken care of... and rest. Please write down any thoughts or comments you may have here:

_____

_____

_____

_____

QUESTION 2:

Are you still worried or concerned? If so, continue to write down your concerns. And we'll talk about it tomorrow. Today, rest. Please write down any thoughts or comments you may have here:

_____

_____

_____

_____

QUESTION 3:

There is nothing that you and I cannot handle together. Today, please rest. Please write down any thoughts or comments you may have here:

_____

_____

_____

_____

DAY 15

Financial Truth

What have you been telling yourself financially? Is it making you rich…rich beyond your wildest dreams? Or is it making you worry, and/or putting you into debt? Now, you may ask me, St. Anthony, to find your financial truth. Here is your financial truth. And it *is* rich. You see, it all comes from us. This is the truth.

Now, if you have debt, see its truth. Who told you that unpaid bills were your truth? Now ask me, St. Anthony, to find your truth. I can do this for you. And now, you are free. After all, I am the Saint of all lost things.

Today,

Be truthful with your money. Be financially truthful with yourself.

The truth is that it all comes from G-d.

Now you know the truth. And the truth will set you free.

QUESTION 1:

Where did you think your money came from? Are you surprised by your answer? How did it feel? Please write down any thoughts or comments you may have here:

_____

_____

_____

_____

QUESTION 2:

Where would you like your money to come from? How does this feel? Please write down any thoughts or comments you may have here:

_____

_____

_____

_____

QUESTION 3:

In the truth, there is no fight. What would happen if you stopped fighting for; or; about money? How would this feel? Now you are living in your truth. Are you smiling? Please write down any thoughts or comments you may have here:

_____

_____

_____

_____

BONUS QUESTION:

What would happen if you stopped talking badly, complaining, or feeling bad about money? How would this feel? Please write down any thoughts or comments you may have here:

_____

_____

_____

_____

DAY 16

Mistake(s)

I made a mistake today. I didn't write Day 16. I skipped right over it. And I moved onto Day 17. As I am going over each day, I realized that I didn't write this day.

When you make a mistake, do not automatically judge yourself and beat yourself up over what you think, or thought: you may have done wrong. Ask yourself if you harmed anyone in the process.

If you have not harmed anyone, you may forgive yourself and move on to deciding what action you need to do, if any, to correct the mistake.

I am correcting my mistake by rewriting this page for you. There was no harm done at all.

If, on the other hand, you did harm or hurt someone with your mistake, you may honor that you hurt someone and, if possible, make amends or apologize to whoever you hurt. If you hurt yourself via your mistake, again, apologize to yourself for hurting yourself. And now you will be able to have a place within to make better choices from.

You see, when you make a mistake, you can now look at the effect you've had on yourself and others. And now, you can make a different choice. I will be able to find that new choice for you. After all, I am the Saint of All Lost things.

Today,

Did you make a mistake today? If not, please do not blame yourself for the mistakes of others.

Their mistakes had nothing to do with you or what you did or may have done.

QUESTION 1:

Did you notice how you are no longer blaming yourself? After all, most of our mistakes do not hurt anyone. How does this feel? Please, write down any thoughts or comments you may have here:

_____

_____

_____

_____

QUESTION 2:

Can you *let go* of thinking that anything *you* may have done; is responsible for someone else's actions or mistakes? If so, you are well on your way to living in financial joy. How does this feel? Please write down any thoughts or comments you may have here:

_____

_____

_____

_____

QUESTION 3:

Financial joy is not something you receive. It is the place in which you live. This place comes from within. How does this feel? Please write down any thoughts or comments you may have here:

_____

_____

_____

_____

DAY 17

Living Financially from Your Heart

And now, you are able to see your financial choices from a loving place. You are now living financially from your heart. This is an amazing financial place to be. I am excited to show you all the financial love that is there! I'm excited that you have chosen to explore new ways of financially loving, living, and experiencing your life. I am so very proud of you.

If you're not sure how to do this, you may ask me, St. Anthony, to find your financial-loving choices. And I will bring you more financial joy! This is part of the financial joy. Thank you for allowing me to find it for you. After all, I am the Saint of all lost things.

Today,

Try this…

If you are upset about a financial situation, put your hand on your stomach.

Now, put your hand on your heart and tell yourself, "I made the right choice today."

You may also ask me, St. Anthony, to find you the right choice or solution today.

QUESTION 1:

What would happen if all your financial choices came from a place of loving yourself? How would this feel? Please write down any thoughts or comments you may have here:

_____

_____

_____

_____

QUESTION 2:

Some of you (and you know who you are) like a good challenge. You may set yourself up in a situation by creating a good challenge to overcome. This is not loving. How does this feel? Please write down any thoughts or comments you may have here:

_____

_____

_____

_____

QUESTION 3:

Did you remember that I, St. Anthony, am always here to assist you? What would you like me to find for you today? And if I found it for you, did you know that I sent it with love? How does this feel? Please, write down any thoughts or comments you may have here:

_____

_____

_____

_____

DAY 18

Financial Blessings

Are you ready to Bless others with your financial Blessings? Just say to yourself or out loud, "Today, I will share my financial Blessings with others."

If you are still concerned about money, this is okay too. Just say to yourself or out loud, "St. Anthony, please find me *one* financial Blessing." And; I will. After all, I am the Saint of all lost things.

Today,

Look for the financial Blessings in All.

Just say to yourself or out loud, "This situation Blesses or Blessed me Financially."

QUESTION 1:

Did you want to curse your financial situation? Or, can you see the Blessing in it now? How does this feel? Please write down any thoughts or comments you may have here:

_____

_____

_____

_____

QUESTION 2:

If you do not see the Blessing(s) in this situation, you may ask me, St. Anthony, to assist you by finding you MONEY! I bet you thought I was going to say Blessings! How does this feel? Please write down any thoughts or comments you may have here:

QUESTION 3:

Please keep on asking me, St. Anthony, to bring, locate or find money for you. Or better yet, ask me to bring you financial joy! I love doing this for you. How does this feel? Please write down any thoughts or comments you may have here:

_____

_____

_____

_____

BONUS QUESTION:

I, St. Anthony, would love to bring you financial joy. Why: on earth; would I bring you money if it didn't bring you joy? How does this feel? Please write down any thoughts or comments you may have here:

_____

_____

_____

_____

DAY 19

Financial Hoarding

Do you hoard? Are you a hoarder? Or do you give freely? If you use the word "when," you are a hoarder, always waiting for that one rainy day when you might actually find the thing you put away for that- rainy day.

You cannot hoard and expect to feel Blessed. When you hoard, you live in dread. How can that ever Bless you or anyone else?

If you are a "hoarder" or if you are using the word "when," replace the word "when" with the word "now."

Today,

What are you saving that you might need later?

You might be saying that you need to have a savings account. This is different. A savings account is your investment in you.

This is not for a rainy day; this makes you feel secure.

Today, let's trade hoarding for feeling secure.

You have just become human. It is human to have humility. It's a great virtue.

Congratulations!

QUESTION 1:

Do you feel financially secure? If not, you may ask me, St. Anthony, to find you financial security. This is part of Financial Joy and Bliss. How does this feel? Please, write down any thoughts or comments you may have here:

_____

_____

_____

_____

QUESTION 2:

Now, doesn't that feel better. I knew it would. Please write down any thoughts or comments you may have here:

_____

_____

_____

_____

QUESTION 3:

Did you notice that you were no longer thinking about rainy days at all? It was my, St. Anthony's, Honor to find this for you. How does this feel? Please write down any thoughts or comments you may have here:

_____

_____

_____

_____

DAY 20

Financial Alignment and Attraction

You are now becoming aligned and able to attract more of what we want to give into your life! How does this feel?

I, St. Anthony, am very Proud of you today!

Thank you for letting all of this in!

Today,

Think about what you would like to allow, or bring, into your life.

Did you remember to ask for it?

QUESTION 1:

Alignment is your natural ability to receive. Alignment tells you that everything is in its right order. How does this feel? Please write down any thoughts or comments you may have here:

_____

_____

_____

_____

QUESTION 2:

As you allow more of what we would like to give you, you naturally become more aligned. Now, there is no guesswork. How does this feel? Please write down any thoughts or comments you may have here:

_____

_____

_____

_____

QUESTION 3:

What else would you like your new alignment to bring into your life? Please remember to ask for it. I will bring it or something better. How does this feel? Please write down any thoughts or comments you may have here:

_____

_____

_____

_____

DAY 21

Rest

Rest in knowing that we are already taking care of you in your new alignment.

Enjoy being taken care of by us today.

Rest.

Today,

Enjoy this aligned, joyful day of rest.

QUESTION 1:

Today, Rest. Allow this new alignment energy to replenish and rejuvenate you.

_____

_____

_____

_____

QUESTION 2:

If you would like, think of all the things we have given you so far! And rest.

_____

_____

_____

_____

QUESTION 3:

There is nothing you need to do that we do not know about. Please rest. We'll talk again tomorrow.

_____

_____

_____

_____

DAY 22

Financial Tithing

Financial Tithing is a way of giving back. As new money comes into your life, you must give back. This creates a financial "flow." As you give, it is given unto you. So, when you give, expect you will be taken care of and that more money will be added to you. This benefits your life in two ways: 1) You become one with the flow of MONEY. 2) You will no longer have financial fear. All financial fear is removed as you give and expect new money to come into your life. Pick a charity or a worthy cause for your financial tithing. Then, watch the financial abundance appear!

Today,

Count how many times you gave generously today.
Count how many times you prospered today.
Financial Joy includes prosperity or feeling abundant.
Count how many times you felt "abundant" today.

St. Anthony

QUESTION 1:

What makes you feel abundant or prosperous? Now, ask yourself if these things make you feel financially joyful. Please write down any thoughts or comments you may have here:

_____

_____

_____

_____

QUESTION 2:

Are you ready to create financial joy? If so, please ask me, St. Anthony, to find a place for you to put it. This is your rightful place. Your rightful place includes a place for your financial joy. How does this feel? Please write down any thoughts or comments you may have here:

_____

_____

_____

_____

QUESTION 3:

You have just found your financial rightful place. Are you complaining? If not: Enjoy! If so, what would you like that would make it more joyful (or right)? How does this feel? Please write down any thoughts or comments you may have here:

_____

_____

_____

_____

DAY 23

Your Rightful Place

Your rightful place is filled with financial joy! It has more money than you could spend in a lifetime. You feel supported. And you feel valued.

If you are not feeling supported or valued, you may ask me, St. Anthony, to bring you the support you need right now.

You may also ask me, St. Anthony, to bring you more things to appreciate. Appreciation adds value.

Today,

Remember to appreciate all.

Then watch to see who or what appreciates, or, adds value to you.

QUESTION 1:

What would your rightful place look like? How would it feel? It feels valued, loved, and belonging. Please write down any thoughts or comments you may have here:

_____

_____

_____

_____

QUESTION 2:

If you would like, think of a person who you value. And, then, tell this person that you appreciate them. Sometimes, we may think that we value someone, but we may not tell them. So, today, if possible, tell one person that you appreciate him or her. How does this feel? Please write down any thoughts or comments you may have here:

_____

_____

_____

_____

QUESTION 3:

I, St. Anthony, appreciate and value you. You may ask me, St. Anthony, to find ways to add to your life. How does this feel? Please write down any thoughts or comments you may have here:

_____

_____

_____

_____

DAY 24

Financial Inspiration

What inspires you? Did you know that I, St. Anthony, inspired Shira, the author, to write this book? She will become a millionaire through the sale of these books! She doesn't like to talk about that.

What, if anything, are you inspired to do today? If you're not sure, you may say to yourself or out loud, "St. Anthony, please inspire me by finding ideas for me that will bring me joy!"

Did you notice that I didn't say "Financial Joy"? This is because financial joy is part of your joy! You just never saw it this way! How fun is that?!

Today,

Be inspired to find joy! Be inspired to be joyful!

QUESTION 1:

If you were inspired to find financial joy, would you see it as a new job, or more money? Or would you just allow me, St. Anthony, to find you new inspirational ideas? Please write down any thoughts or comments you may have here:

_____

_____

_____

_____

QUESTION 2:

Did you know that when you act on your inspirations or ideas, you can create? Did you know that this brings me, St. Anthony, Great joy? How does this feel? Please write down any thoughts or comments you may have here:

_____

_____

_____

_____

QUESTION 3:

Did you know that you cannot feel Blessed, inspired, and deprived at the same time? Now, see or imagine any thoughts of "lack" or "not having" disappearing, as you are inspired to feel financially Blessed and joyful. How does this feel? Please write down any thoughts or comments you may have here:

_____

_____

_____

_____

DAY 25

Financial Tidbits

Here are a few:

1) If you ask, you shall receive. You may not receive what you "expected." You see, here, we only give you the best!

2) If you are feeling any sense of lack, you may ask me to find you. Just say, "St. Anthony, please find me."

3) If you would like to ask me, St. Anthony, to find something for you, you may now tell yourself that you were inspired to ask for this item, or for this help.

4) And remember that I, St. Anthony, love you.

Today,

Ask to be inspired to receive more from us.

QUESTION 1:

What is your new financial tidbit that you would like to share? Did you know that you were inspired to do this? How does this feel? Please write down any thoughts or comments you may have here:

_____

_____

_____

_____

QUESTION 2:

If you saw a tidbit as a treat, what would you treat yourself to today? Would you like it? Please write down any thoughts or comments you may have here:

_____

_____

_____

_____

QUESTION 3:

If you saw your tidbit as an inspiration, what would you do with it? Would you use it once? Or would you use it to take the first step to create something so much better, and so much greater? Thank you for allowing me to inspire you. Tidbits are bits and pieces of inspiration. And it was my, St. Anthony's, pleasure to do this for you. How does this feel? Please write down any thoughts or comments you may have here:

_____

_____

_____

_____

BONUS QUESTION:

Sometimes, we use tidbits to inspire others, instead of knowing that as we inspire others, we are actually taking the steps that are leading us to the next better place in our own lives. For, as we give, we are given. How does this feel? Please, write down any thoughts or comments you may have here:

_____

_____

_____

_____

DAY 26

Financial Heaven

Financial Heaven. What would that even look like to you? Or better yet, how would it feel? If you don't know, would you like to find out? I can show you. Now see yourself there. Picture all the people in your life who are on the sidelines cheering you on! This is Financial Heaven. And I can bring it all to you. After all, I am the Saint of all lost things.

Today,

Describe in detail what Financial Heaven would look like or feel like to you.

Now, see the first person you called to tell them you are there!

QUESTION 1:

You cannot be in Financial Heaven and not share it with others. Who is the first person you called to share your Financial Heaven with? Please write down any thoughts or comments you may have here:

_____

_____

_____

_____

QUESTION 2:

Now, see this person (from Question 1) in their own Financial Heaven. How are you supporting or cheering them on? How does this feel? Please write down any thoughts or comments you may have here:

_____

_____

_____

_____

QUESTION 3:

Did you know that the way you support and cheer on this person (from Question 1) is also part of how you Bless them? How does this feel? Please write down any thoughts or comments you may have here:

_____

_____

_____

_____

DAY 27

Time

If you had more money than you could spend in a lifetime, how would you use your Time? Are you a workaholic? For a workaholic, there is never enough Time.

What would happen if Time became the commodity or the thing you wanted more of instead of money?

Now, you are able to see the value of your Time.

You and your Time are valuable.

Today,

If you saw your time as valuable, how much money would you have?

If these two (time and money) do not seem to go together right now, don't worry, they will.

QUESTION 1:

How would it feel if your time and money got together? Please write down any thoughts or comments you may have here:

_____

_____

_____

_____

QUESTION 2:

Now, just say to yourself or out loud, "I have more than enough time and money." What, if anything, changed? How does this feel? Please write down any thoughts or comments you may have:

_____

_____

_____

_____

QUESTION 3:

Allow this into your life. You can do this by asking me, St. Anthony, to find you the money and resources you need right now. How does this feel? Please write down any thoughts or comments you may here:

_____

_____

_____

_____

DAY 28

Rest

Rest. Drink plenty of water and rest.

Okay, you're learning how to get more time, or to take the time you need and deserve.

Rest.

DAY 29

A Few Alignment Exercises

Here are a few Alignment Exercises we thought you might enjoy:

1) Shira, The Author, drives a Blue Car. When she is driving, she tells herself that, for every blue car she sees, she has an extra $100.

And then she starts counting – First Blue car – she has an extra $100. Second Blue Car, she has an extra $200. She does this until she gets to $1000.

Then, she switches the color and starts again. She may look for white cars.

And she will tell herself: for every white car she sees, she has an extra $100 and so on...

You may try this using any denomination of currency that works well for you.

2) This is similar to the first exercise. Shira, the author, likes to collect Angel figurines. She tells herself that, for every angel she sees in her home, she has an extra 100 dollars. And, then, she starts to count her angel figurines:

The first angel she sees, she tells herself she has an extra $100.

The next angel she sees, she has an extra $200.

And so on...

What do you collect or have a lot of? Now say to yourself or out loud, for each of these items that I see, I have an extra $100 (or whatever denomination of currency that works well for you.)

You may continue this until you finish seeing these items.

3) Read completely and then try this exercise: If you drive a car, sit down, close your eyes, and picture yourself as a multimillionaire, and see yourself sitting in your new car. What color is it? What color is the interior? Now, look in the middle of the steering wheel and see the letters, emblem, or symbol. What type of car is it?

When Shira did this exercise, she saw herself sitting in a Blue Car with a Black interior. The Letters in the Middle of the Steering wheel were BMW. She now owns that car.

Today,

Have fun using these different techniques to align with having money and Financial Joy!

QUESTION 1:

Sometimes, we do not need to do anything. If you are waiting for "results," consider doing one of the exercises we suggested today. Please write down any thoughts or comments you may have here:

_____

_____

_____

_____

QUESTION 2:

If you liked a particular day of this book, use it as often as you would like! This is my, St. Anthony's, gift to you. How does this feel? Please write down any thoughts or comments you may have here:

_____

_____

_____

_____

QUESTION 3:

Feel free to use any exercise or technique that works well for you. And remember, it's always supposed to make you feel better or good. You know it's working when it feels good! How does this feel? Please, write down any thoughts or comments you may have here:

_____

_____

_____

_____

DAY 30

Thank You

I wanted to think of the Perfect way to thank you.

I wanted you to know how important and valuable it is to be you!

I wanted to tell you how much I love you.

Did you hear it? Did you feel it?

I am Wishing you the Best in All on Your Journey - St. Anthony.

Today,

Please continue to feel the Love I, St. Anthony, am sending your way.

And please continue to ask me, St. Anthony, to find you things that will bring you more Joy and Financial Joy.

And, of course, thank you for reading this work.

You Bless me ~ St. Anthony

Blessings, Love and Light,

St. Anthony

QUESTION 1:

If there was one more thing you could ask me, St. Anthony, to find for you, what would it be? Did you know that asking me for things has opened you up to receiving? How does this feel? Please write down any thoughts or comments you may have here:

_____

_____

_____

_____

QUESTION 2:

If you would like, please pick a charity or organization to give back to. You will add value to their efforts! How does this feel? Please feel free to write down any thoughts or comments you may have here:

_____

_____

_____

_____

QUESTION 3:

You have just become part of something bigger! Congratulations are in order! How does this feel? Please write down any thoughts or comments you may have here:

_____

_____

_____

_____

Please continue to ask me, St. Anthony, to continue to find your lost items or to intercede upon your behalf.

If you would like to start this book again, please feel free to. Each time you read this work, you may get something new from it!

You may also want to go back to a particular page that you enjoyed, as well.

Sent to you with Love – St. Anthony

DAY 31

Letting in Financial Love

Will you let in financial love? What part of your financial situation is not full of love or loving? If you have an answer, you may ask me, St. Anthony, to find financial love for you. You see, when you have a way of loving yourself, it will include how you treat yourself with money. And, then, you can ask me, St. Anthony, to treat you well with money. And I will. This is my promise to you. You see, it all comes from G-d. Just say to yourself or out loud, "G-d, Universe or Spirit, please Treat me well with money." You see, when G-d Treats you well with money, you have financial love. And I, St. Anthony, can find this for you. After all, I am the Saint of all lost things.

Today,

How you treat yourself is how you are treated.

Ask to be Treated Well with money.

Just say to yourself or out loud, "I treat myself and others well."

Now, say to yourself or out loud, "I treat myself and others well with money."

Say to yourself or out loud, "G-d, Spirit or Universe: Thank You For Treating Me Well With Money." And, "I am enjoying all of my rewards."

QUESTION 1:

How did you treat yourself with money today? Did you treat yourself well? If so, how did it feel? Please write down any thoughts or comments you may have here:

_____

_____

_____

_____

QUESTION 2:

If you did not treat yourself well with money, no need to worry. Just do the opposite and see what happens. You may also ask me, St. Anthony, to find you new ways to treat yourself well with money. How does this feel? Please write down any thoughts or comments you may have here:

_____

_____

_____

_____

QUESTION 3:

If you treated yourself well with money, what's the next nice thing you would do for wonderful you? Did you notice that it may not have anything to do with money at all? How does this feel? Are you smiling? Please write down any thoughts or comments you may have here:

_____

_____

_____

_____

Yes, this was the perfect way to end this book.

Thank you again,

St. Anthony

ABOUT THE AUTHOR

Shira Plotzker is a Psychic, Medium, and Pet Communicator. She has been doing readings professionally for over 20 years. Shira has been featured in the *New York Times*, www.Newsweek.com and The NY Post. She was a columnist for *The New Jersey Herald*.

What People Are Saying About Shira's Work

"Is my wife going to get pregnant?"

Shira replied, "Get pregnant? You're going to have Triplets!!!"

Two weeks later, guess what? We're having Triplets!

Thanks, mam - R.Q.

We love to hear comments from readers. Please send correspondence to Shira at P.O. Box 307, Nanuet, New York 10954, or email: shirasplace@gmail.com

You may also schedule a session with **Shira via her website: WWW.SHIRASPLACE.COM**

As far as choosing me for your Patron Saint, remember if you choose me, St. Anthony, I will give you voice. If you choose another Saint to be your Patron Saint, I'm sure they will be honored. If you are not ready to choose a Patron Saint, remember, we are all here to assist you. And you can call upon us always. We are here for you!

Printed in Great Britain
by Amazon